Telling Tails

Photography , poetry and musings
of an Alberta farm girl

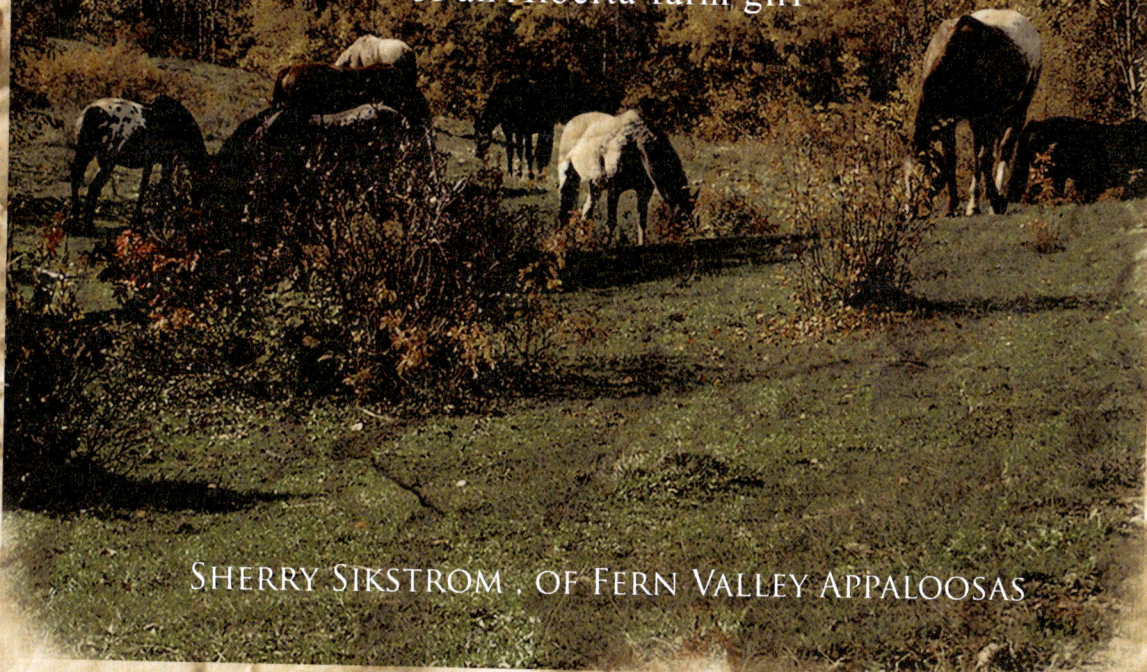

SHERRY SIKSTROM , OF FERN VALLEY APPALOOSAS

Order this book online at www.trafford.com
or email orders@trafford.com

Most Trafford titles are also available at major online book retailers.

Printed in the United States of America.

ISBN: 978-1-4269-6657-6

Library of Congress Control Number: 2011906572

Trafford rev. 05/05/2011

Trafford
PUBLISHING® www.trafford.com

North America & international
toll-free: 1 888 232 4444 (USA & Canada)
phone: 250 383 6864 ♦ fax: 812 355 4082

Telling Tails
Photograghs ,Poetry and Musings
of an Alberta farm girl
By
Sherry Sikstrom
Of Fern Valley Appaloosas
Unforgettable Spots

This book is dedicated to my loving family and friends, who have supported me and encouraged me through my life to reach for the stars and to follow my dream.

And also dedicated to the wonderful creatures who have graced my life, and fed my life long love affair with horses.

Telling tails

If I wrote a book,
What would it be?
Adventure or romance
Or a great Mystery?
No if I wrote a book,
It would be my story
In verse and in rhyme
Just simple, no glory
But mine all the same
About who I am
Nobody special
With no real plan
Just what I've done
And where I have been
Where it began
What's yet to be seen?
No big ships
With billowing sails
Just my life
And a few Telling Tails

My story and history with horses and Appaloosas

I first wrote this essay to accompany photographs taken by Linda Finstad of "A Sharper Image Photography" This and the photographs will be housed in the Alberta Archives Museum ,as a part of the "Equine Heritage Project" I was greatly honored and humbled to be asked as one of the Alberta horse breeders to participate in this wonderful project .

I was raised on a mixed farming operation north of Edmonton, Horricks Dairy. The family has had horses throughout the history of the farm , with my grandfather using drafts to deliver milk in the 30's then lighter saddle horses used for cattle work, gathering the herds and, for a time herding the cattle through the old streets of Edmonton and out to the grazing land at Ministik Lake . I developed a love of horses early on and learned to ride on the "ranch broke" horses used on the farm. At the age of 12 I felt I had saved enough baby sitting money and my wages from washing milk bottles , to buy my very own horse . My Dad drove me out to a little town called Picardville, where my love affair with Appaloosa horses began. I tried a mare by the name of Gloalta Toyogha, a liver chestnut with a roan blanket. After trying her we left to "think it over" and as we drove away; she was in a turnout along the road, she galloped along beside us, true poetry in motion! Dad and I agreed then and there, she was it! We returned to the farm, paid for her and I took her home on my 13 birthday May 02, 1981.
We ran for miles her and I, then in the following spring it became apparent I was going to be the owner of 2 appaloosas! Sherry's April Sunshine arrived April 09 1982.
Over the years I continued to nurture my love of horses and especially Appaloosas, raised a young stallion, Chile Poivre. I was advised that "little girls can't handle a stallion, he will just get mean." Prove them wrong? Oh yeah! Chips was the sire of many of what are now known as Fern Valley Appaloosas , and in all the years I had him he was a perfect gentleman, never needing more than a growled "mind your manners."
Primarily we raise Appaloosas here for light saddle horses. They are an incredibly versatile breed. The Alberta Challenge of the Breeds is proving

that time and again with Team Appaloosa often winning the contest! Although the need for "ranch horses" has lessened in the past 50 years or so with the reduction in herds and the advent of ATV products, many of us still use them for farm /ranch work. Also the horse industry remains strong in that pleasure riding is a popular pastime as are cattle penning, Gymkhana, jumping, endurance riding etc.

The Appaloosa has come a long way from its origins as the Nez Perce Horse, primarily owned by the Nez Perce tribe along the Palouse River (Snake River) in Washington and Idaho. These were tough horses bred to run and to go into battle, or to be hunted off of, bright loud colors and markings, often little or no mane and tail, strong hard "striped feet."

The breed suffered a setback, as outlined below:

"In the late 1800s, war broke out between the U.S. Calvary and the Nez Perce Indians. The Appaloosa was the reason the U.S. Calvary was deprived of victory for many months, as the Nez Perce fled over 1300 miles of rugged, almost impassable terrain under the guidance of the famed Chief Joseph. The final defeat of the Nez Perce came in Montana. They surrendered their horses, left them behind, or they were distributed amongst the settlers. The proud band of carefully selected horses was gone."

Many were bred to draft or destroyed; they slowly came back, but in the process some of the "originality" was lost. They have been crossed with Quarter horse and Thoroughbred, but the true Appaloosa characteristics' often shine though; White sclera, around the eye (giving it a "human" look) mottled skin, striped (laminated hooves) and of course the myriad of coat patterns that they are famous for!

My hope for the future of the breed and all horses in Alberta is that they continue to thrive and bring joy to horse enthusiasts as they have with me for so many years. The days of the "working horse" are not yet gone and with cutting, roping, endurance, gymkhana, pleasure riding and driving etc, I believe there is an incredible future ahead for these horses. Also more specifically the Appaloosa breed to remain true to its origins and for them to maintain the remarkable individuality and integrity that makes them Appaloosas. My love affair continues.

The Horses

I have had an enduring love of horses my entire life, and at the age of 13 scrimped and saved till I could afford to buy my very first horse. An Appaloosa mare named Gloalta Toyogha . She was the beginning of a life long love affair with the Appaloosa breed.

My good mare (Gloalta Toyogha)

An Appaloosa? Really?
They are just stubborn and silly
She doesn't have a pretty head
"You don't ride that part "I said
She was sweet and kind, and fast
The skepticism didn't last
For when they saw her run that day,
They didn't have a thing to say
My first horse, and my first love
A gift for me from up above
Not always was she good as gold
But she taught me well, and made me bold
She was the foundation of my herd
And that good mare got the last word!

Sherry's April Sunshine

Early on one April day
Nestled in with straw and hay
Snug in the old Dairy barn
My April Sunshine was born
A leggy Chestnut filly there
That little one, she knew no fear
From her birth to the day she died
Sunshine was never one to hide
First foal I raised, my oh my!
She gave to me my very first black eye
And broke my nose, I should mention
But not by her unkind intention
We did some learning she and I
Bred to run, oh she could fly!
Descended from Triple Crown stock
In a race she couldn't be caught
She grew up tall and strong, and white
It seemed she changed overnight
A gentle horse, quiet and staid
She calmly walked through a parade
I could call her anywhere
Across the fields to me she'd tear
And stop up close and quietly stand
Checking for cookies in my hand
In later years she lost her sight
But still my Sunshine shined so bright
Raised up some foals of lovely stature
Watching her was pure rapture
Gone from me now,
Yet still somehow
In my heart she'll stay
And no one really ever can
Take my Sunshine away

1 11 2003

11

Chips (Chile Poivre)

You'll never manage him they said
Just a kid ,I hung my head
He'll just get mean as he gets old
They all do I was told
A frustrated child I hung my head
Your just a kid, you can't they said
But in my head I formed a plan
He and I would show that man
And work we did
To make him mind
And at the shows he brightly shined
He could dance and be a ham
Heart of a lion, kind as a lamb
His legacy now an affirmation
To good old try and determination
His offspring grand and colored loud
With heads held high, they do him proud
He never did get mean as crud
Not my Chips, not my old stud

Chilleens Catana

In the spring, you came to me
Just two kids, in fact were we
As we grew and as we learned
In faith and trust, a bond we earned
Through the years, you taught me well
Oh the stories we could tell
You gave me wings, you let me Fly
And helped me learn to truly try
The mountains climbed, the rivers crossed
And miles of trails, yet never lost
Beautiful, and kind, were you
Stalwart, strong, a heart so true
Never asking me for much,
A pat a hug, a gentle touch
And then in your advancing years,
You healed my heart, and faced my tears
Always there, you never strayed,
And in my heart, you have stayed
In the fall we said goodbye
Falling leaves and a clear blue sky
So difficult so let you go
But it was your time, this I know
From the beginning, and until the end,
You were my heart, my Horse my friend

They First Called her Ashes

They first called her Ashes
But that was just Silly
Ashes was no name for that
Little grey filly

—

A pretty rough start
For that little girl
But she showed she had heart
And gave us a whirl
A new owner soon
Who started to see
Just what
That little grey mare could be

—

You sure couldn't push her
Or force her to bend
But with patience and
Time
She gave in the end

Stubborn and stoic
Tireless and strong
She'd give what she got
And go the day long
She made me a friend
Lasting and true

—

And though I wouldn't admit it,
I loved her too
A stealthy horse,
In shadowy state
Before you would see her
She would slip out the gate
Time marched along
Just like it does
And we are left wondering
Just where it goes
From Ashes she came
To Ashes she went
But the time in between
Was brilliantly spent

—

She runs through my mind,
Now and again
Like the warm southern wind
That gave her a name

The horses in my life continue to inspire me every day , this poem ,is written for my current saddle horse,There are many more , and as time goes along I hope to write more of their stories , but for now this is the last one dedicated to a horse of mine.

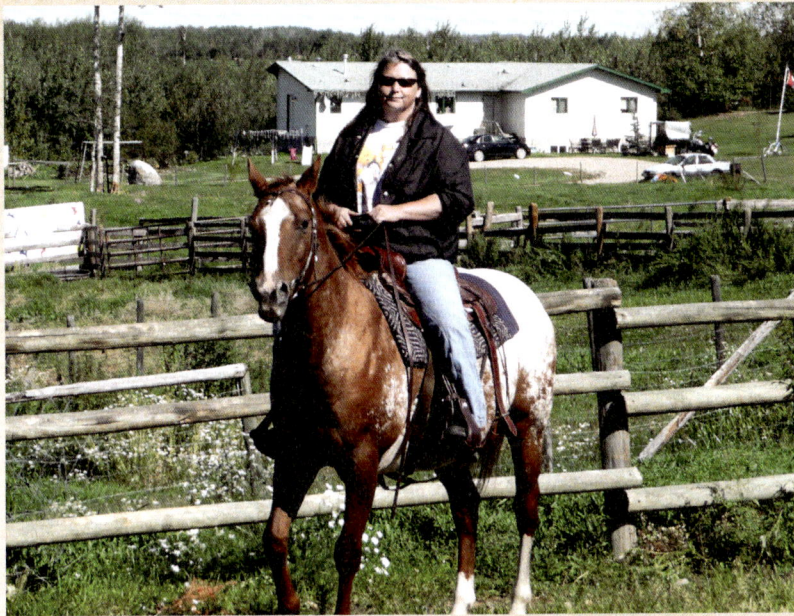

Johnnie

Under an old Spruce tree
Beside a pond and rock
A little mare, Miami Mouse
Went out for a walk
Away from home and her safe herd,
She chose to be alone
And there in the quiet space,
She had her little one
A copper red, with lots of chrome
And a blanket white as snow
Lying there beneath the tree the trouble didn't show
But when he stood to take a drink
Sadly what did I find?
For on 3 legs that crippled colt,
One twisted in behind
His back leg seemed short and wrong
And didn't touch the ground
I couldn't see how possibly
he could come around
The vet, and my own dear dad said,
wait and bide my time,
As he could stand and eat
So wait I did, but worried still
that we would face defeat
For 3 long days I checked on him,
and it was worth the wait
When on the fourth the little mare
brought him to the gate
His little leg, though still not right
was brushing along the ground
And I knew right then and there,
he would someday be sound
He grew up strong and sweet and good,
a brave horse, worth a ransom
And who was he? This crippled colt?
His name is Johnnie Handsome

In this life we meet many people , and yet sometimes the animals have a greater impact . In this case it is, and was the other way. While I will always remember the horse . It was the man got my attention . This is about and for my husbands good horse Rowdy.

The old timer

Old already when we met
But still a horse I won't forget
Swollen knees and graying hair
But if you knew the horse in there.
Before the damning signs of age
When he was young, and centre stage
Rowdy was my husband's horse
A bright chestnut and fast of course
Not an easy ride I hear,
Some memories are fraught with fear
Many races run just fine
A rider, or not at the finish line
But when he came to live here
The old man had lost a gear
His retirement, it was grand, grazing on the lush green land
Winter came, and into the barn,
Where we kept the old man warm
Fed him mush and he limped along
Bright eyed but thin the winter long
And in the spring ,with the sun
On pastures green how he did run
3 good days, then with the dawn ,
I woke to find that he had gone
In the place that he liked best,
In soft green grass he laid to rest

Each and every horse I have been blessed to know or work with has touched my life and impacted me in some way . For the ones I have yet to know or write about ,I will close this chapter with the following poems.

Give me a horse

Give me a horse
With good heart and mind
Yes give me a horse
And I'll find the time
Give me the knowledge
To manage his care
To teach and to train
In a manner that's fair
Give me the space
And days in the sun
To first learn to walk,
Then learn to run
Give me the push
To do what I need
To earn both our keep
And pay for his feed
Give me the courage,
When he's done his best
When his time is done
To put him to rest
Leave me the horse
In my mind and heart
The joy and the memories
Right from the start
Yes give me a horse
And I'll do the rest
As he does for me
I'll give him my best

Made of Horses

For my entire life it seems
Horse have been in my dreams
In my life and in my space
A feeling that you can't replace
The Grace and beauty that they share
Cannot be found, just anywhere
They are a thing second to none
To let them go leaves me undone
And heartbroken tears I will cry
When all to soon they say goodbye
Each takes a piece of my own heart
When the sad time comes to part
But leaves behind no empty space
Just glowing memories in their place
I watch them grow and watch them dance
And know that it was worth the chance
No rage against natures forces
It has left my heart
Made of Horses

Catch Me a dream

To Catch a Dream
How fleeting, they are
On the tip of you mind
Yet away, oh so far
As we lay down to sleep
And rest for the night
Some wonderful dreams
Often take flight
And once in a while
When wide awake
A life of their own
These dreams can take
I dreamed of a horse,
A particular one,
who would bring back to me ,
my days in the sun
Not exactly the same ,
The differences clear
But of spirit and heart
Of one I hold dear
Catch me a dream
And in wonder I stand
Can she and I do
All,I have planned ?
A wandering muse
Deep in the night,
To Catch a Dream ,
And watch it take flight

On Farm Life

As I have said , I was raised on a farm , and I continue my life in the country . It is not the easiest life , but one I truly love .I grumble and struggle by times, but at the end of the day I wouldn't trade this lovely life for the world.

Alberta farm

"Life on the farm,
Is kind of laid back"
Not!!!
Freezing cold ,or screamin' hot
Alberta farm girls, a fact we know
Can shovel grain, and shovel snow
With winds strong enough to take your hair
For the livestock, we feed and care
Frozen hands, or sunburned necks
We do this all, not for a cheque
But for the simple joys it seems
Of horses cows, and cowgirl dreams
Hauling hay and packing pails
Any wonder we spike our Ginger ale?
Balance this, with miles of beauty
Makes it all a lighter duty
The calves the foals, they frolic in
The lush green fields where they begin

—

And then the weather, again it turns
With howling winds, with cold it burns
Who would trade this cushy life?
For City lights and gang war strife
Not me, I'll take the frozen feet
And all the beef that I can eat

33

The Farmer

He comes into town
In his old rubber boots
The marks of the years on his face
His hands gnarled up,
A bend to his back,
a bit of a hitch in his pace
He moves a bit slow,
but steady he goes
For he knows life isn't a race
He ruined his back
To save a sick calf
One of so many it seems
He worries and fights
On those long winter nights
Colder and colder it seems
Then fencing and seeding and
All of the rest
No holidays, to speak of
He gives it his best
This is the farmer, the man of the land
The fellow who gives all he has
And they do it why honey?
Well it ain't for the money
The glory, the fun, or the tan
They do it for family,
and they do it for pride.
And simply the love of the land.
And into the fall, he answers the call
For harvest and weaning and such
When all this is done, he is the one
To quiet a horse with a touch
So give him respect,
a handshake or a nod
Or even a pat on the arm
The food that you eat
and the shoes on your feet
They started somewhere on a farm

Spring has sprung,
The winter done
At least that's
What they say
I looked outside
And nearly cried
Instead of green grass showing
In typical Alberta fashion
I woke to find it snowing
I will take heart,
On this bleak day
As spring will surely come
My way
It takes a little longer,
yet ,with it we grow stronger
and eager for the change
The snow and cold, it sure got old
A tough one , this long year
We long for days
Of sunny haze
Hard work and ice cold beer
Soon the green will come again
To bless this patch of heaven
And we can all sit back and smile
We survived the winter of "11

Calving Season

Calving time is now upon us
Though I complain I must be honest
When I see the calves so dear
I really like this time of year
Extra time and lots more duties
But watching all those little beauties
It seems worth it in the end
As springtime comes to us again
As each new calf comes to us
We hope for very little fuss
But if there's trouble
Out we will go
Cold or wet we won't say no
Pulling a calf or bottle feeding
We're here to give them
What they're needing
And though we give it our best try
There are some that still will die
Sad and oh so disappointing
Yet no finger of blame is pointing
Grab a twin if you can
And graft it on is a plan
Or maybe buy a Holstein cross
To help to mitigate the loss
When all the calves are on the ground
Gather them up one time around
Tag and brand vaccinate
Then send them out through the gate
Cut 'em loose onto the grasses
Let them grow as summer passes

What's in a name

Cowboys and Cowgirls
I've heard some say
Live a rough kind of life each day
Ridin' ropin' cuss and spit
Work all day and never quit
For me that doesn't fit so well
When I get mad I can yell
I try hard to watch my mouth
But you know
When things go south…
I can ride, but I don't spit
And frankly, I can't rope for…
Nothin'
But we have cows, well that's a given
And its part of how I make my living
These days it's not all that easy
To live the country life
I work in town, during the day
In the evenings throwing hay
Checking cows, at calving time
We get supper, round half past 9
I don't dress up, in boots and hat
More often sweats and a ball cap
I have good dogs and good horses
And I stand against the cold winds forces
I feed and watch and care for cows
I guess that qualifies somehow
Makes me a cowgirl, or maybe not
But a name is just a name, its true
Whatever I am, I guess I'll do

Elusive Louie

Let me tell you a story ,
It might make you laugh
A story about a renegade calf
mystical magical , runs like a deer
It seems there is one of them every year
I will see him once , on the day he is born
then find myself searching every morn'
This kind of calf , wont let you be lazy
by the time he is done, he will make you crazy
Now you will see him.
nope you don't, now
he is gone in an instant
nobody knows how
After 2 hrs of searching the entire farm
in total exhaustion you throw up your arms
"I guess he's a goner , no more to be done
You will find him lying right next to his mom !

Random thoughts on life , love and living well

Thoughs and musings in verse , some funny, others melancholy .But each from my heart.

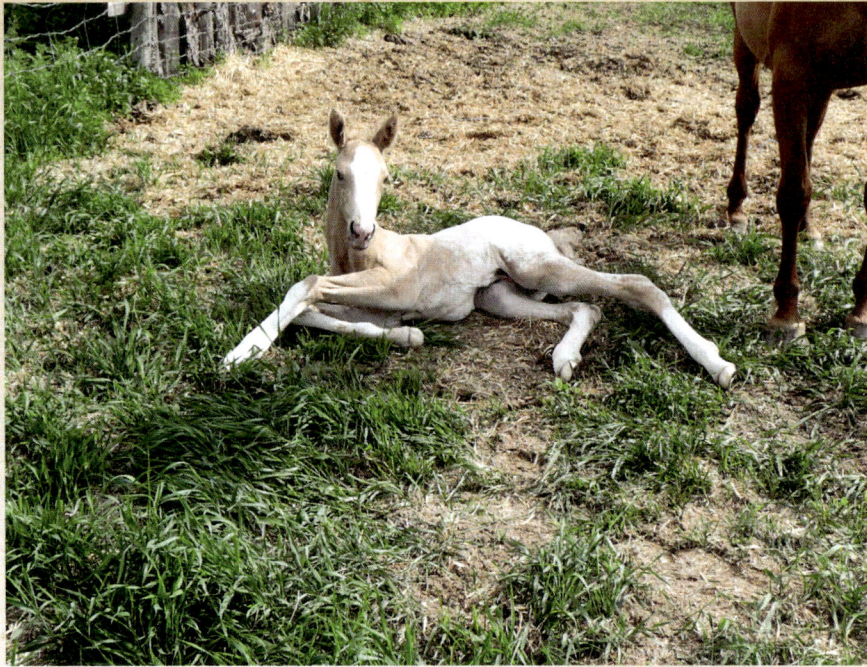

Gamblers life

This life it is a gamble sure
At least that's what they say
the life we live , is what it is
each and every day
Some were meant for Violins
And some dance to a fiddle
others still are happy to be
Somewhere it the middle
Live it wise and live it well
There are no second chances
Enjoy this life for all it is and
Take those second glances
Have adventures if you can
Memories to carry in your hand
Share the wealth,
Enjoy good health.
It doesn't stay forever
And words you may not want to say
Are, can't and won't and never
Who you are, what you become
Are choices you have made
Its not the cards that you were dealt
It's simply how you played

Ruts

Some days are not so great
Nothing really wrong
But still I feel at odds
The entire day long
Any thing I try
Nothing seems to fit
I 'm not gonna lie
Some days I want to quit
Just the kind of day
You can't take any more
And I start to feel
Like a dog stuck in a cat door
On that kind of day ,
I take another route
Or maybe ask a friend
To come and let me out

When Lonely comes to call

It doesn't give you warning
You might not understand
Afternoon or in the morning
When Lonely comes to call
It takes you by surprise
As the tears begin to fall
Never see it coming
When Lonely comes to call
All the insecurities
You thought you left behind
All the words left in your mind
That took your confidence
Although you don't believe them
Suddenly make sense
You are too plump
Not pretty enough
Not at all like your sister
Come on now be tough
If you would only …
Cut your hair or learn to dress,
Lose that weight, stand up tall
Come on straighten up'
Why are you such a mess?
When Lonely comes to call
These are the things
That comes spinning back
Suddenly your heart feels under attack
In a room full of people

Or all on your own
When Lonely comes to call
It's a funny thing
That what we do
to each other
In the guise of care
No one sees the effects
Not father sister Mother
Remember my dear
Those words aren't real
If you don't give them power,
Your heart they can't steal
Turn lonely into solitude,
And enjoy the quiet time.
Reflect on all that you
Have become, and
What you have left behind
And remember when
All is said and done
You my friend are worth it
Put your faith in God above
He believes you are perfect

A bad day??

At the end of the kind of day, where it all falls apart
And you need to complain, but Lordy! Where to start?
Slept in late, never ate, the car was dead as dirt
Spilled your coffee, on your blouse, stubbed your toe it hurt!
Work was tough, couldn't get it right
The whole long day, you tried, but ,such a fight
And then back home, the supper burned
A day you felt you hadn't earned
You just want to yell and scream
"Why did I have this day",
Or was it just a dream
At the close of such a day,
before you say good night
Don't think about what went wrong
Just remember what went right

House or home

A house is mostly built of wood
Built up strong, in hopes it would
Defy the winds of natures rage
And keep you warm though your old age
But a home is built, with heart and tears
Where you share your love and fears
Living life as family strong
The place you feel that you belong
What the difference is you ask
To explain it is a simple task
Those who truly have a home will know
You take it with you wherever you go

Prayers

When I would bow my head at night
And fold my hands in prayer
I sometimes used to wonder
Who would hear and care
As life has brought me to this day
Good and bad along the way
I try to stand strong in faith
And let God lead the way
A lesson often fought against
But must be learned I guess
Our prayers are always answered
It just isn't always yes

To catch a dream

To catch a dream ,
Is a task that I know
To catch a dream,
You must let go
Not to give up ,or
To leave it behind
But free it to grow
Not just in your mind
A dream held too tight
Will smother and die
But held to the light
Oh! then watch it fly
Nurture your dreams
And bring them to light
Then send them up
And let them take flight
So set your dreams free
To see them come true
With time faith and work
They will come back to you

Get a bit wild

Get a bit wild,
If you are able
Act like a child
Dance on a table
Revisit your youth
Don't just be boring
Tell a bad joke
Leave them all roaring
Flash them a smile
Give it your best
There is plenty of time
Later to rest
Forget to be stiff,
Uptight and staid
At the end of the day
Make sure you have played

Holiday's end

Under a palm
In the Mexican sun
The feeling of
Nothing but time
A beautiful place
The sun on my face
The tropical flowers, divine
But all good things it's said
Must come to an end
And though it was fun
The holiday is done
So good bye to the sun
And the sand,
The sights of this tropical land
And home to the snow,
I am ready to go
I will come again
But never too long
Although she gets cold,
Home never gets old
Alberta is where
I belong

For we two

Take my heart and take my hand
On that day we made our stand
To see it through, thick and thin
The days we'd lose and ones we would win
We had our dreams
And set them free
Some came true,
Some not to be
We have had some fights you and I
And then made up, by and by
Struggles that seemed to last forever
We get through them all together
And though our plans and dreams have changed
Hopes for children, rearranged
I believe we'll make it through
We are enough, just we two

The Holiday Season

Christmas past

The holidays have come and gone
And the march for spring begun
Today I smile and yawn
And think of what we've done
Family friends, food and wine
Parties, visits galore
Each of them were oh so fine,
And seemed to lead to more
But now the call to reality says,
Though all the goods were yummy
Before we start the working days

I will sit and rub my tummy

Resolutions

Every year we resolve
To improve or to evolve
Quit that habit lose some weight
Run a gambit Go on a date
Live it wild take a chance
Yell and shout Sing and dance
Shoot the moon go for glory
Or maybe just tell my story
Live each day in a fashion
That's caring, kind
And shows my passion
And at the end of every day
Know that I can truly say
I'm not perfect, I'm just me
But the best darn me that I can be!

New Years and Laundry

There are wives tales of old
That are some hard to believe
Like the one, laundry must be done,
By midnight New Years Eve
It's passed from mom to girls,
To caution us with fear
That if it isn't done by then,
It won't be done all year
Well I will have to look at the chance
And go ahead and take it
For me to get my Laundry done,
I'd have to party naked!

Be Kind

Treat each person every day
In a fashion and a way
That won't make you take a second look
If they ever write a book
Imagine, in a new release
To be the villain of the peace
You never know whose muse will wake
And what direction it will take
I you are careful and are kind
There won't be cause to look behind
At the damage you have done
When that book hits # 1

1 11 2003